Mel Bay Presents

Ballads & Songs of WWI

by Jerry Silverman

Visit us on the Web at http://www.melbay.com — E-mail us at email@melbay.com

THE FIRST WORLD WAR
1914-1918

© C. S. HAMMOND & Co., Maplewood, N.J.

The Allies
Neutral States
Advances of the Allies

The Central Powers
Areas Occupied by
the Central Powers
Advances of the Central Powers

EUROPE AND THE
NEAR EAST

SCALE OF MILES
0   100   200   300   400   500

Stabilized Line on the
Western Front, 1914-1917
Eastern Front on the Eve of the
Russian Revolution, Oct. 1917
Limit of Allied Advances
in the East
Area Occupied by the Central
Powers after Brest Litovsk
Treaty, 1918

THE WESTERN FRONT

SCALE OF MILES
0   20   40   60   80

Limit of German Advance, 1914
Limit of Trench Warfare, 1914-1917
Hindenburg Line, 1917
Limit of Final German Advance, 1918
Armistice Line, November 11, 1918
Limit of Allied Occupation Zone

Courtesy New York Public Library

Contents

From Tin-Hat Alley To Tin-Pan Alley

> Give me some hardtack,
> Give me some cheese,
> Give me a crust of bread,
> And let me eat my fill
> Of old corn Bill,
> And call me well fed.
> Don't give me eggs or ham,
> But lots of strawberry jam,
> And brew me some tea;
> And if you have an army shoe,
> Just stick it in the stew;
> And if you run short, Pat,
> Cook up my old Tin Hat,
> And leave the rest to me.

This bit of soldiers' doggerel was written by an American doughboy whose outfit was joined to a British division in France and who was living on British rations. It is a typical soldiers' complaint about the army food you love to hate. It is also a far cry from many of the wartime songs that were being written back home, with lines like "Mother's sitting knitting little mittens for the Navy." In fact, there were two parallel streams of songs being created during the course of "the war to end all wars" — one by the soldiers "over there" and the other by songwriters "over here."

In 1912, two years before the "guns of August" started their deadly cannonade along the western front, British songwriters Jack Judge and Harry Williams composed a lighthearted song about a young Irishman who debarks in London seeking his fortune. It was a typical "Irish" musical hall number about a stereotypical "Paddy" who leaves his "Irish Molly-o" behind. He writes her of the wonders of the big city, but it is clear that his heart remains with her back home in...Tipperary. Who could have imagined at the time that two years later, literally millions of young Irish, English, Canadian and American soldiers would have picked up the catchy refrain of "It's A Long, Long Way To Tipperary" and transformed it into *the* marching song of the war.

If one of the purposes of a soldier's song is to lift his morale and get his mind off the horrors that surround him, then "Tipperary" filled the bill to a T.

The American counterpart to "Paddy" was "Rube" just off the farm, who found himself transported 3,000 miles across the ocean (an ocean he may never have seen before). Shot at and gassed, living in muddy trenches, eating lousy food and himself being food for lice, he, too, longed for home. But there was something else on his mind as well: Gay Paree! The mysteries of the French language and wiles (real and imagined) of the "mademoiselles" had a profound effect on him.

"Parlez-vous" became a catchword for all things French. Never mind that it was some-times spelled "parley-voo" — spelling didn't count, just feeling. Just as "Tipperary," written two years before the war, was sung up and down the lines, "How Ya Gonna Keep 'Em Down On The Farm After They've Seen Paree?" — written one year after the war — summed up "Rube's" nostalgia for a Paris that changed his outlook on life.

But what of the real war and its horrors? How did songwriters react to the fact that millions of men were engaged in a cataclysmic life-and-death struggle? If we are to judge by the titles in this collection (and they are typical of the hundreds and hundreds of wartime compositions), there is an air of unreality about many of them. Written in the Tin-Pan Alley musical idiom of their day, so many of them are lively, bouncy, raggy "Broadway" tunes describing humorous situations set off with clever rhymes. For every "serious" "In Flanders Fields The Poppies Grow" or "On The Somme Front," there are dozens of frivolous "When Yankee Doodle Learns To Parlez Vous Français" and "Sister Susie's Sewing Shirts For Soldiers."

The formulaic eight-bar introduction and the two- or four-bar repeated section ("Vamp" or "'Til ready") that invariably precedes the singer's entry (during which the performer may ad-lib some "bits of business" before the audience) comes straight out of the vaudeville/ music hall tradition. Indeed, show-biz composers like George M. Cohan ("Over There") performed their wartime compositions before enthusiastic audiences at Liberty Bond rallies and other patriotic gatherings, making an easy transition from fluff to fervor.

Not that humor has no place in a wartime setting. There is a long tradition of military griping, making light of misery and, of course, poking fun at the enemy in song.

When, during the Revolutionary War, British General John Burgoyne's forces were defeated by American General Horatio Gates and his men at the Battle of Saratoga on October 7, 1777, insult was heaped on injury by the Vermonters who had taken part in the fight:

> In seventeen hundred and seventy-seven,
> General Burgoyne set out for heaven;
> But as the Yankees would rebel,
> He missed his route and went to Hell.

Guerre 1914-15-16... Dans la SOMME
Offensive Française - Canons pris aux "boches"
57me Série

War 1914-15-16... In the SOMME (E.D)
French offensive - Guns taken from the Germans
Visé, Paris No 1416

After a British naval squadron had ineffectively bombarded Stonington, Connecticut, on August 9, 1814 (during the War of 1812), Philip Freneau ("The Bard of the Revolution") dashed off "The Battle Of Stonington," which contains these lines:

> They killed a goose, they killed a hen,
> Three hogs they wounded in a pen;
> They dashed away — and pray, what then?
> That was not taking Stonington.

And when on May 10, 1865, fleeing Confederate President Jefferson Davis (supposedly disguised in women's clothing — but wearing his riding boots) was captured by Union forces, it did not take long for "Jeff In Petticoats" to appear in print. The last verse of that song (words by Henry Tucker, music by George Cooper) skewers Davis with outrageous puns:

> The ditch that Jeff was hunting for,
> He found was very near;
> He tried to "shift" his base again,
> His neck felt rather queer;
> Just on the out-"skirts" of a wood
> His dainty shape was seen,
> His boots stuck out, and now they'll hang
> Old Jeff in crinoline.

But the Civil War also gave us "The Battle Hymn Of The Republic," "Tenting On The Old Camp Ground," "When Johnny Comes Marching Home" and the spiritual "Free At Last."

Army food, ever the bane of the poor soldiers' existence, has always offered fertile ground for pungent imagery. During the Spanish-American War they sang:

> The peas they was greasy,
> The meat it was fat.
> The boys was fighting Spaniards,
> And I was fighting that.

Another taste of military cuisine of that time was offered by Joe Hill, better known as the composer of militant labor and political songs. In his song "Stung Right," he takes ironic aim not only at the naive young man who joins the navy "to see the world," but at the Armour meat packing company, whose spoiled cans of beef supplied to U.S. forces were the cause of a notorious scandal.

> Some time ago when Uncle Sam he had a war with Spain,
> Not many of the boys in blue were in the battle slain.
> Not all were killed by bullets, though — no, not by any means.
> The biggest part that died were killed by Armour's Pork and Beans.

Honorable Discharge from The United States Army

TO ALL WHOM IT MAY CONCERN:

This is to Certify, That* *William Silverman*

† *600,228* *Private*

THE UNITED STATES ARMY, *as a* TESTIMONIAL OF HONEST AND FAITHFUL

SERVICE, *is hereby* HONORABLY DISCHARGED *from the military service of the*

UNITED STATES *by reason of* ~~Authority Contained~~ *End of emergency.*
A. Y. after Nov 23/8

Said William Silverman was born

in ————, in the State of London, England

When enlisted he was 21 years of age and by occupation a Clerk

He had Grey eyes, Black hair, Ruddy complexion, and

was 5 feet 2½ inches in height.

Given under my hand at Camp Abraham Eustis this

third day of Dec, one thousand nine hundred and Eighteen

Ticket form *P-2* No. *33606*
from *Richmond* to *New York*
Issued hereon *12/3/18* ———191—

E. L. Frant Pr. ½ C.

Commanding.

To be sure, not all professional songwriters regarded World War I as some kind of cakewalk, "on ze boulevard" of Gay Paree. British composer Ivor Novello's "'Til The Boys Come Home (Keep The Home Fires Burning)," with lyrics by Lena Guilbert Ford, is as moving an appeal to the home front's stiff upper lip as anything ever written in any war. And for stirring marches, nothing beats George M. Cohan's "Over There."

Sentimental tear-jerkers are also well represented, with little girls picking up the telephone and asking "central" to connect them with daddy in France or in no-man's land while mama quietly sheds a tear nearby.

For anti-war sentiment in song, nothing ever expressed it better than "I Didn't Raise My Boy To Be A Soldier," written in 1915. When America finally entered the war in April 1917, however, songs like that were submerged by numbers such as "Good-Bye Broadway, Hello France!" and Irving Berlin's "Let's All Be Americans Now."

Canadian songwriter, entertainer and pianist Gitz (Ingraham) Rice joined the Canadian Expeditionary Force at the outbreak of the war. He fought in many major campaigns and was invalided at Vimy Ridge in 1917. Neither his active service nor his wounds interfered with his songwriting and his supervision of entertainment for the troops. Three of his songs are included herein: "I Want To Go Home," "Keep Your Head Down, 'Fritzie Boy'" and "We Stopped Them At The Marne" (which in addition to enumerating a number of major battles also contains some strongly expressed anti-pacifist lines).

Poets were as affected by the war as songwriters. Alan Seeger, serving in France, wrote these prophetic lines:

> I have a rendezvous with Death
> At some disputed barricade
> When Spring comes round with rustling shade...
>
> And I to my pledged word am true,
> I shall not fail that rendezvous.

A little late for his spring rendezvous, Seeger was killed in action July 4, 1916.

Débarquement des troupes Américaines.
Disembarkment of American troops

"THE BEST COMFORT"

In 1918, Carl Sandburg, reflecting on the insane futility of all wars wrote:

> Pile the bodies high at Austerlitz and Waterloo.
> Shovel them under and let me work —
>   I am the grass; I cover all.
>
> And pile them high at Gettysburg
> And pile them high at Ypres and Verdun.
> Shovel them under and let me work.
> Two years, ten years, and passengers ask the conductor:
>   What place is this?
>   Where are we now?
>
>   I am the grass.
>   Let me work.

9

Another musical look at the at the war is supplied by the songs written by the soldiers themselves. As might be expected, they present a more realistic view of life "over there." There may be an occasional "parley-voo" or "ooh la la" — to keep up appearances — but they are more concerned with everyday details like snipers, lice, mud and German machine guns. The doughboys of Tin Hat Alley saw the war from a different perspective than the dough boys of Tin Pan Alley.

Black American soldiers, in particular, brought a special musical idiom with them to France: the blues. Using the flexibility of the blues, they were able to combine specific wartime statements, such as, "I'm goin' to Germany," or "Scratch your lousy back," with more traditional lovin'-and-leavin' lyrics. The U.S. Army's jim crow segregationist policy — all-black units commanded by white officers — is reflected in songs like "Diggin'," which describes the kind of work to which they were generally assigned.

British soldiers had their traditional "tot o' rum" to lift their spirits. The French kept warm with their *vin rouge* (or *blanc*). But when American soldiers, who had gotten used to the more permissive European attitude toward alcoholic beverages, returned home in 1919, what greeted them? Prohibition! "I've got the blues...since they amputated my booze," they wailed in "The Alcoholic Blues." No wonder they missed Gay Paree! Down on the farm, or in the big city. But that's another story...

The ballads and songs of World War I, then, represent more than just a frozen slice of life lifted from the second decade of the twentieth century. Springing from the national psyche, most enjoyed immense popularity in their day. They were and are, first and foremost, *songs* meant to be *sung,* and were chosen here as much for their musical value as their historical significance. With some transpositions and other minor modifications, the Tin-Pan Alley songs are presented in their original arrangements. Guitar chord symbols have been added to make them more accessible to a wider public. Most of the Tin-Hat Alley songs appear here for the first time with piano arrangements.

Finally, we are left with this eternal question:

Would you rather be a colonel with an eagle on your shoulder,
Or a private with a chicken on your knee?

Courtesy Sid Glickman collection

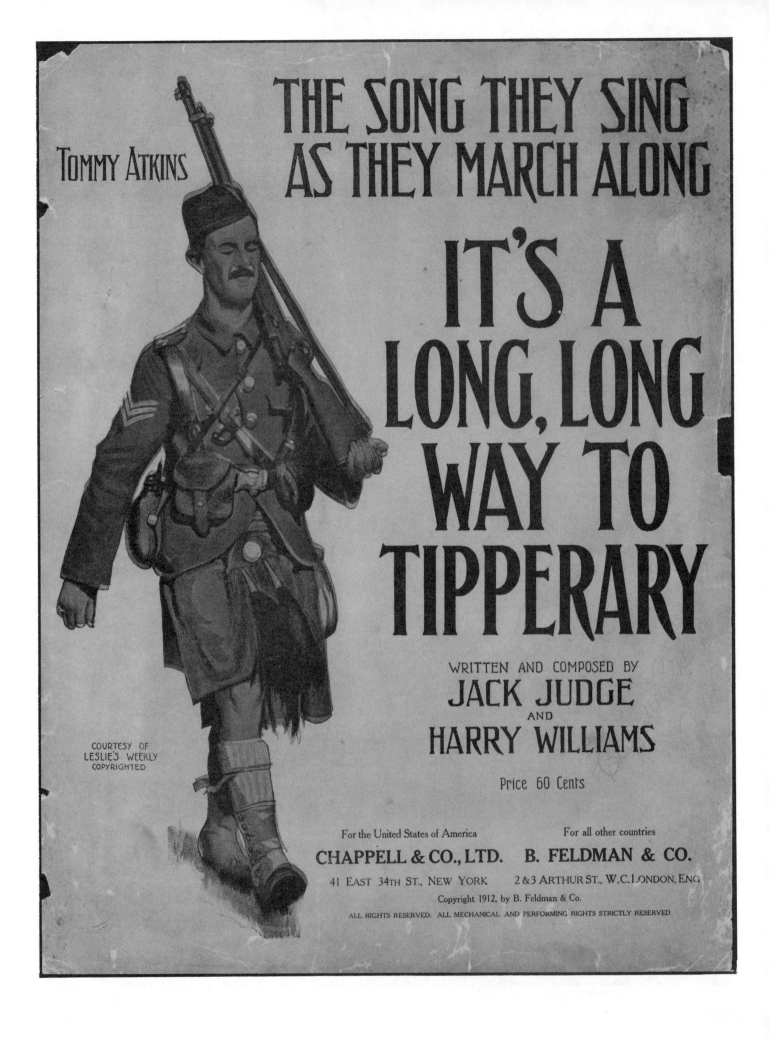

THE SONG THEY SING AS THEY MARCH ALONG

Tommy Atkins

IT'S A LONG, LONG WAY TO TIPPERARY

WRITTEN AND COMPOSED BY

JACK JUDGE

AND

HARRY WILLIAMS

Price 60 Cents

COURTESY OF
LESLIE'S WEEKLY
COPYRIGHTED

For the United States of America   For all other countries

CHAPPELL & CO., LTD.   **B. FELDMAN & CO.**

41 EAST 34TH ST., NEW YORK   2 & 3 ARTHUR ST., W.C. LONDON, ENG.

Copyright 1912, by B. Feldman & Co.

The Song They Sing As They March Along
It's A Long, Long Way To Tipperary
(1912)

By Jack Judge & Harry Williams

Up to migh-ty Lon-don came an I-rish-man one day,
Pad-dy wrote a let-ter to his I-rish Mol-ly O',
Mol-ly wrote a neat re-ply to I-rish Pad-dy O',

As the streets were paved with gold, sure ev-'ry-one was gay,
Say-ing, "Should you not re-ceive it, write and let me know!
Say-ing, "Mike Ma-lon-ey wants to mar-ry me, and so,

Singing songs of Piccadilly, Strand and Leicester Square, 'Til
If I make mistakes in spelling, Molly dear," said he, "Re-
Leave the Strand and Piccadilly, or you'll be to blame, For

Paddy got excited, then he shouted to them there:
member it's the pen that's bad, don't lay the blame on me."
love has fairly drove me silly, hoping you're the same."

Chorus

"It's a long way to Tipperary, It's a long way

to go; It's a long way to Tipperary,

14

To the sweet - est girl I know! Good - bye, — Pic - ca - dil - ly, Fare - well Leices - ter Square. It's a long, long way to Tip - per - ar - y, But my heart's right there!" there!"

We Take Our Hats Off To You, Mr. Wilson!

(1914)

By Blanche Merrill

You're one of Un - cle Sam - my's boys, You have no use for
Un - cle Sam is might - y proud, He's proud he picked you

an - y noise, You've won ev - 'ry Yan - kee heart from coast to coast;_____
from the crowd. He's_____ proud that you have shown the world your worth._____

Great - er than a glad - i - a - tor, you're the world's big
You've sought peace with ev - 'ry na - tion, Steered us through all

med-i-a-tor, On you, this whole U-nit-ed States can
trib-u-la-tion, And made our land the great-est land on

boast._____ We'd trust you in an-y kind of fuss;_____
earth._____ You've set up a stan-dard for the world,_____

We're glad you be-long to us._____
The flag of peace you've un-furled._____

Chorus

We take our hats off to you, Mis-ter Wil-son,_____ Our

17

home and a-broad, Your pen is great-er than the sword; We take our

1. hats off_____ to you.

2. Your you._____

Four years after this song was written, President Woodrow Wilson arrives in Paris in November 1918 for the signing of the Versailles Peace Treaty. He is seen here escorting Madame Poincaré, the wife of the French president, at the Bois-de-Boulogne station after the arrival of his special train from the port of Brest. Courtesy New York Public Library

The War In Snider's Grocery Store
(1914)

By "Hank" Hancock, Ballard Macdonald
and Harry Carrol

Hans Gus - tav Sni - der, A lo - cal pro - vi - der Of
Dutch pum - per - nick - le Had joined a dill pick - le, At -

gro - cer - ies, canned goods and such, Had read of the war, 'Til him -
tack - ing the fresh na - vy beans. A lim - burg - er cheese Great - ly

self and the store Were both what is known as "In Dutch." His
strength - ened the breeze, And an - cho - vies, prunes and sar - dines Were

G   B7

brains he'd been feed - ing On   so much war read - ing,   He
fight - ing an ar - my Of   da - go sa - la - mi,   And

C   G   D7   G   Ddim   D7

woke up one night— in a fright.   He rushed down the stairs,— Fell—
that's on - ly half— what he saw.   He jumped in - to bed,— Put—

G   Gdim   D7   G   Gdim   G7   *Chorus* G#dim

o - ver two chairs,— And turned on the gro - c'ry store light: There were
ice on his head,— And went on the wag - on once more:

A7   Adim   A7   D7

egg - shells burst - ing near and far,— A - bove the Russ - ian ca - vi - ar.— A

Bis - marck her - ring by it - self__ Was push - ing all the French peas

off the shelf.__ An I - rish po - ta - to start-ed to cry,__ When a

Span-ish on - ion hit its eye.__ Frank-furt - ers fight - ing all o - ver the floor,__

Howl - ing and growl - ing, "We're the dogs of war."__ There was

"Sun - ny Jim,"— up - on a horse, Swoop - ing down— with all his "Force." The pap-

ri - ka grow - ing weak - er, shout - ed out:— "Won't you o - pen that door?"—— And a

cou - ple of tough Vi - en - na rolls— Shot a poor Swiss cheese all full of holes,— In the

ter - ri - ble war— in Sni - der's gro - c'ry store——— —

23

Courtesy New York Public Library

'Til The Boys Come Home

(Keep The Home-Fires Burning)

(1914)

Words by Lena Guilbert Ford　　　　　　　　**Music by Ivor Novello**

They were sum - moned from the hill - side, They were called in from the
Ov - er - seas there came a plead - ing, "Help a Na - tion in dis -

glen, And the coun - try found them read - y At the stir - ring call for
tress!" And we gave our glo - rious lad - dies; Hon - or bade us do no

men. Let no tears add to their hard - ship, As the
less. For no gal - lant son of Bri - tain To a

There's a sil - ver lin - ing Through the dark clouds shin - ing.

Turn the dark cloud in - side out, 'Til the boys come home. *Fine*

D.C. al Fine

Result of a German zeppelin bombardment of a house in England. Courtesy New York Public Library

Sister Susie's Sewing Shirts For Soldiers

(1914)

Words by R.P. Weston

Music by Hermann E. Darewski

Sis - ter Su - sie's sew - ing in the kitch - en on a "Sing-er," There's
Piles and piles and piles of shirts she sends out to the sol - diers. And
I for - got to tell you that our sis - ter Su - sie's mar - ried, And

miles and miles of flan - nel on the floor and up the stairs. And
sail - ors won't be jeal - ous when they see them, not at all. And
when she is - n't sew - ing shirts, she's sew - ing oth - er things. Then

It May Be Far To Tipperary

It's A Longer Way To Tennessee
(1914)

Words by Arthur J. Lamb

Music by Alfred Solman

Com - rade, the drums are beat-ing, My heart is beat - ing too.
Com - rade, the sun is set-ting, My life is set - ting too.

Com - rade, the bu-gle's greet - ing Calls us to die or do!
Com - rade, don't be for - get - ting What I have asked of you:

Com - rade, you have a sweet-heart On Er - in's Isle you say. But
Tell her, I had to leave her. Don't let it break her heart; For

may be far to Tip-per ra-ry; It's a long-er way to Ten-nes-

see! see!

Courtesy New York Public Library

I Don't Want To Go To War

(1914)

Words by Edward Madden

Music by Henry I. Marshall

Good-ness Mer - cy! Lis - ten, Per - cy,
Shades of Pha - roah! Think of ae - ro -

Hear the bu - gles call!   Find a place to crawl,
plan - ing in the sky!   Dropp - ing from on high,

From the can-non ball.
Bon-bons in your eye!

I'm so ner-vous, Lord pre-serve us!
Flags are pret-ty, what a pi-ty

Must we vol-un-teer?
They should be shot at. *(Bang!)*

I'll keep in the rear. I'll
Heav-ens, what was that? A

wave the flag and cheer,
bul-let through my hat!

"Hoo-ray!
That's why,

Go 'way!
"Good-bye!"

Come
Shall

Chorus

back some oth-er day!"
be my bat-tle cry.

I don't want to go to war!

35

scream! _____

My fa - ther named me How - ard, I'm so
Let them hol - ler, "How he flies!" In -
I met Theo - dore Roo - se - velt, He

glad that I'm a cow - ard. I don't want to go to
stead of say - ing, "Here he lies!" So
said, "You could not lick a smelt!" So

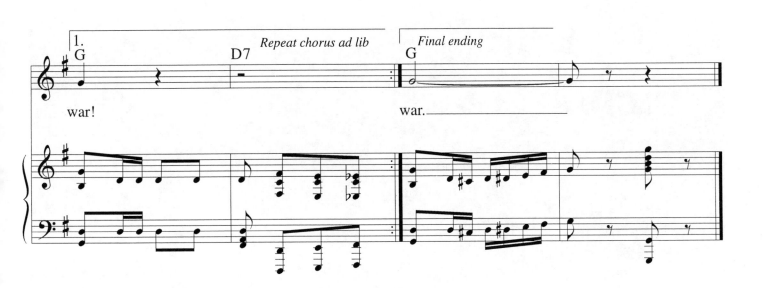

Repeat chorus ad lib   *Final ending*

war!   war. _____

37

Courtesy New York Public Library

Courtesy New York Public Library

Written at the Battle of Ypres

I Want To Go Home

(1915)

By Lieut. Gitz Rice
1st Canadian Contingent

Vamp 'til ready

When first I joined the Ar - my, not so
meas - les I have suf - fered, and had

ve - ry long a - go, I said, "I'd fight the foe, And help Sir Doug-las Haig*, you
twelve at-tacks of "flue," And "men - in - gi - tus," too; But then, no one ev - er

know." I've been in France just six - teen months, and fight-ing now as yet, I
knew. The rain and mud has giv - en me "Me - di - tus" of the spine. I

*Field Marshall Sir Douglas Haig (1861-1928), commander in chief of all British forces

Alleman(ds): French for "Germans"

I Didn't Raise My Boy To Be A Soldier

(1915)

Words by Alfred Bryan

Music by Al. Piantadosi

Ten mil - lion sol - diers to the war have gone, Who may nev - er re - turn a - gain._____ Ten mil - lion moth - ers' hearts must break For the ones who died in vain._____

What vic - to - ry can cheer a moth - er's heart, When she looks at her blight - ed home?_____ What vic - to - ry can bring her back All she cared to call her own?_____

Head bowed down in sor - row In her lone-ly years, I heard a moth-er
Let each moth-er an - swer In the year to be, Re-mem-ber that my

Chorus

mur - mur thro' her tears:_____ "I did - n't raise my boy to be a
boy be - longs to me!_____

sol - dier, I brought him up to be my pride and joy._____ Who

dares to place a mus-ket on his shoul - der, To shoot some oth - er moth - er's dar - ling

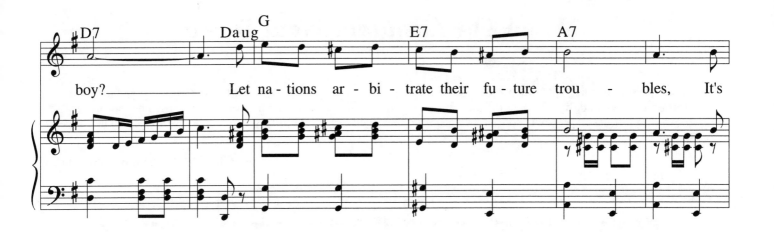

boy?_____ Let na - tions ar - bi - trate their fu - ture trou - bles, It's

time to lay the sword and gun a - way.____ There'd be no war to - day, If

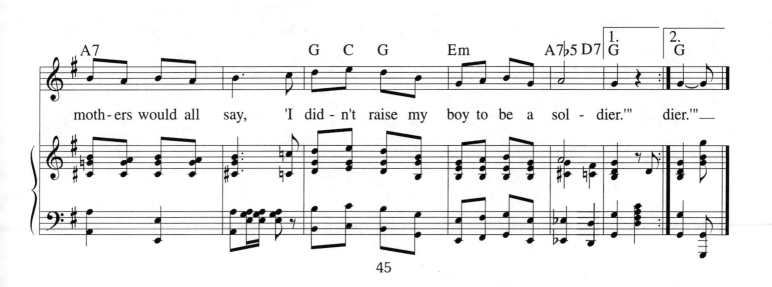

moth - ers would all say, 'I did - n't raise my boy to be a sol - dier.'" dier.'"___

When The *Lusitania* Went Down
(1915)

While attempting to run the German blockade of England on a voyage from New York, the British liner *Lusitania* was torpedoed and sunk by a U-boat off the Irish coast on May 8, 1915, with a loss of 1,189 lives. The Germans apologized, but it was later revealed that the *Lusitania* had been carrying military supplies as well as civilian passengers.

By Chas. McCarron & Nat. Vincent

na - tion is sad___ as can be.___ A mess - age came o -
les - son to all___ it should be,___ When we feel like cross -

ver the sea.___ A thou - sand or more,___ who
ing the sea.___ A - mer - i - can ships,___ that

'Til ready

The

46

ping this war - fare, If wo - men and chil - dren must

drown. Ma - ny brave hearts went to

sleep in the deep, When the *Lu - si - tan - ia* went

1.
down. A down.

2.

49

Courtesy New York Public Library

50

Joan Of Arc, They're Calling You
(1915)

By Frank Sturgis

52

Can't you hear it call - ing too? They real - ly say from your last

breath,_____ That a dove flew to the skies._____ And if

that was the Dove of Peace, Joan__ of Arc, Send it down and dry a moth-er's

eyes. There's a eyes._____

Pack Up Your Troubles In Your Old Kit Bag
And Smile, Smile, Smile

(1915)

Words by George Asaf

Music by Felix Powell

Pri - vate Perks is a fun - ny lit - tle cod - ger, With a smile,____ _ a fun - ny smile._____ Five feet none, he's an art - ful lit - tle dod - ger, With a smile,____ a fun - ny smile._____

Pri - vate Perks went a - march - ing in - to Flan - ders, With his smile,____ _ his fun - ny smile._____ He was lov'd by the pri - vates and com - man - ders For his smile,____ his fun - ny smile._____

Pri - vate Perks, he came back from Bosch - e shoot - ing With his smile,____ _ his fun - ny smile._____ 'Round his home he then set a - bout re - cruit - ing, With his smile,____ his fun - ny smile._____

*Match to light your cigarette

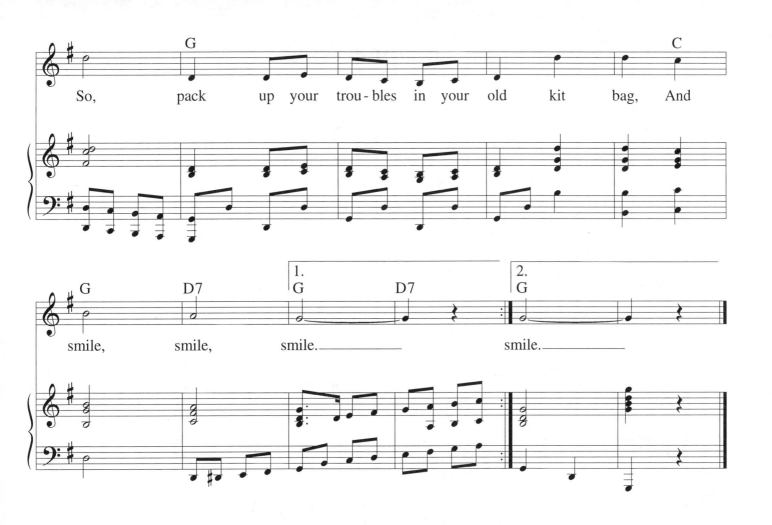

So, pack up your trou-bles in your old kit bag, And

smile, smile, smile. _____ smile. _____

Courtesy New York Public Library

Shrapnel Rag
(1915)

By E. C. Brooke

Hear that shell, Ain't it hell,
Hol - y gee! Look and see

When they start to shoot - ing with the shrap - i - nel! Day and night,___
What a for - ty - cen - ti - met - er did for me. It's all the same,___

in the fight, The boys must keep a - duck - ing to the left and right.
who took aim. I fear for sev - 'ral days I'll be a lit - tle lame.

Dukes and Czars in arm - ored cars, Go - ing to the front a - puff - ing
Ae - ro - planes and arm - ored trains Can - not stand the rack - et where the

"THE EUROPEAN WAR of 1914"
"Repose...arms!!"
"British soldiers training two conscripts of the class of 1930"

Courtesy New York Public Library

We're Going To Celebrate The End Of War In Ragtime

(1915)

By Coleman Goetz & Jack Stern

Ev-'ry-bod-y's ask-ing when_ We will be at peace a-gain,_ Ev - 'ry -
Ev-'ry-one will feel so gay,_ There'll be one long hol - i - day,_ When each

bod-y wants pros - per - i - ty.____ I hear ma-ny peo - ple say,_
na-tion claims neu - tral - i - ity.____ There'll be lots of wav-ing flags,_

Gm D Gm   D7   G7   C

"Lay the sword and gun a-way,"— But still they're fight-ing 'cross the sea.————
Wav-ing to the rag-gy rags,— Each one will have their lib-er-ty,————

Db   Bbm6 C   G7   C   C7

— The end must come, it's true;—— That's why I say to you:——
— With peace in ev-'ry land,—— I trust you'll un-der-stand:——

Chorus
Tacet chords   F   D7

We're going to cel-e-brate— the end of war in rag - time,

G7   C7

Ev-'ry na-tion soon will sing in rag rhyme. Eng-land, France and

63

Ger - ma - ny,— Ev - en folks from I - ta - ly,— The A - ris - to - crats,

And the dip - lo - mats, March-ing arm in arm, See them tip their hats To— a rag - gy mel - o - dy.— (So pret - ty) Ev -

'ry-where there's har - mo - ny.— So when we cel - e - brate— the

end of war in rag - time, Be sure that Wood - row

Wil - son leads the band.   band.

Courtesy New York Public Library

Mother's Sitting Knitting
Little Mittens For The Navy
(1915)

By R. P. Weston & Hermann Darewski

Why is it Pa - pa's fists are al - ways in his trou - sers
day poor Pa - pa said, "Good - bye, I'm going to join the

pock - ets? Why is it that he don't shake hands? Well,
arm - y." The ser - geant looked at him and said, "I

ask him and he'll tell you that he's hold-ing up his pants; There are not an - y
think you are too old, and then, you stoop a tri - fle too." Said Pa, "If you had

but - tons and he dare not take a chance. He has a wife and daugh-ters, all good
pins stuck in your back, you would stoop too. I'm on - ly six - ty sev - en, and I'd

nee - dle wom - en too, But they can't sew on but - tons, They have
glad - ly fight for France; Be - sides, that is the best way to get

Chorus

some - thing else to do: Moth-er's sit - ting knit-ting lit - tle mit - tens for the
but - tons on my pants."

Min - nie winds the wool when they be - gin._____ Sis - ter
Cis - sy's knit - ting socks, and Su - sie's sew - ing shirts for sol - diers, Still, poor
Pa - pa props his Pants up with a Pin._____

1.
— To - Pin._____

Courtesy New York Public Library

Inspired by a Brave Tommy and written at the Battle of Ypres, 1915

Keep Your Head Down, "Fritzie Boy"

(1915)

By Lieut. Gitz Rice

71

Chorus

Courtesy New York Public Library

*"THE SHATTERED VILLAGE OF VAUX, WHERE THE AMERICAN TROOPS BY CAPTURING IT IN FORTY MINUTES
PROVED NOT ONLY THEIR OWN METTLE BUT THE QUALITY OF THEIR LEADERS."*
Courtesy New York Public Library

Somewhere In France
(1916)

By Pvt. Charles Quinn & James Quinn

Some- where in France at the close of a day, Just as the sun tints the
I see the day when he told her "good-bye." I see him kiss her a-

west,___ I see a bat - tle field torn with the fray, And the
gain.___ I see the col - or that flush - es her cheeks, She was

bat - tle - worn sol - diers at rest.___ I see a quaint lit - tle
proud of her sol - dier boy then.___ I see the an - guish that

home far a - way,   Down at the foot of a hill._____
o - ver - comes joy,   I see the hot tears that burn._____ With

I see a moth - er who's fad - ed and gray,   But whose
heart beats that fal - ter she yearns for her boy;   For the

heart throbs with moth - er love still._____
day when he'll safe - ly re - turn._____

Chorus
Tacet chords

Some - where in France_____ Where the shot and shell are scream - ing,_____

76

The Announcer

—From The Herald, New York.

[The Notice on the Bulletin Board is the German Embassy's advertisement giving warning that travellers who sailed on ships of Great Britain or her Allies entering the War Zone did so at their own risk.]

Roses Of Picardy
(1916)

Words by Fred E. Weatherly

Music by Haydn Wood

She is watch - ing by the pop - lars, Col - in - ette with the sea - blue
And the years fly on for - ev - er, 'Til sha - dows veil their

eyes, She is watch - ing and long - ing and wait - ing Where the long white road - way
skies, But he loves to hold her lit - tle hands And look in her sea - blue

lies. And a song stirs in the si - lence, As the wind in the boughs a -
eyes. And she sees the road by the pop - lars, Where they met in the by - gone

Dm7 G7 Gaug C E7 Aaug7 A7

roads   may be far_____ a - part,   But there's one   rose that dies   not in

D9   Gsus9   G7   1.   2.
                                                  C   C

Pi - car-dy!   'Tis the rose   that I keep   in my heart!"   heart!"

D. C.

"Daddy, what did YOU do in the Great War?"
Courtesy New York Public Library

81

Blighty

(The Soldier's Home, Sweet Home)

(1916)

By R. P. Weston & Bert Lee

What's the song the boys are sing - ing out in France? It is - n't
When we get the hap - py news they're home - ward bound, There'll be some

Ten - nes - see, that's not the mel - o - dy.
joy once more up - on the Blight - y shore.

Blighty: Affectionate name for England.

You don't hear them sigh-ing now for Dix - ie - land;
Hear the peo - ple on the quay all shout Hoo - ray!

They've a diff-'rent tune up - on the Arm - y band.
When they see that steam-er com - ing down the bay.

Lis - ten, and you'll hear each gal - lant kha - ki boy
Lis - ten, and you'll hear the mer-ry kha - ki throng

Sing-ing this song___ of joy:_____ Blight-y!
Sing-ing the Home - land song._____

83

in the foam. See that trans - port

read - y to start, Bound for Blight - y, glad to de - part.

Don't you know where Blight - y is? Why, bless your heart! It's the

sol - dier's Home, Sweet Home. Home.

I've Got The Army Blues

(1916)

By L. Wolfe Gilbert
and Carey Morgan

Cheer up, cheer up, cheer up,
Line up, line up, line up,

What's the mat - ter with you? Dry up, dry up,
Hear the Gen - er - al call. Shine up, shine up,

dry your tears___ a - way, I'm wear-y, So drear-y. Leav - ing, griev - ing,
shine your musk - et and sword so trust-y, So rust-y. Knap - sack, horse - back,

part!___ I felt so bad. My old dad-dy and ma-ma too,__

My own sweet-ie was feel-ing blue.__ I've got the Arm-y Blues,__

(Rif-le on my shoul-der) The Arm-y Blues,__ (Boys are get-ting bold-er)

Right a-bout, face a-bout, for-ward march;_ I've got the Arm___y Blues. Blues.

88

Joan Of Arc
They Are Calling You
(1917)

Words by Alfred Bryan & Willie Weston
French version by Liane Carrera

Music by Jack Wells

"New York's 69th Infantry bids the girls goodbye"
Courtesy New York Public Library

Dedicated to the Officers and Men of the 69th Reg't N.G. N.Y.

The Fighting Sixty-Ninth

(1917)

By Anna L. Hamilton

We're not a war-ring na - tion, but we had to take a stand, To
ma - ny of the Six - ty - Ninth have nev - er been to war, But

help the oth - er na - tions and to save our na - tive land. Now Un - cle Sam is
nev - er on a bat - tle - field were brav - er troops be - fore. A - mid the shot and

read - y, read - y for the fray; So he sends the fight-ing Six - ty - Ninth to
shell, they will fight like hell. So give three cheers for the gal - lant boys of the

France to win the day.   They'll fight, fight, fight, be-cause they know that they are
fight-ing Six - ty Ninth.

right. They'll fight, fight, fight, Yes, they'll fight with all their might.   They'll

fight   for the stars   and they'll fight   for the stripes, And they'll fight   for the

o - pen seas.——————— Three— cheers for the Red, White and

Blue.＿＿＿＿＿＿ Three＿ cheers for the Tri - co - lor too.＿＿＿

＿ Yes, they'll fight, they will fight for France with all＿ of their might, And they'll

die for the Red, White and Blue.＿＿＿＿ Now Blue.

Courtesy New York Public Library

Hello Central — Give Me France

(1917)

Words by James M. Reilly

Music by Harry De Costa

A lit-tle girl woke when the dawn was near, And the nurse said, "See your new broth-er, dear." She went to her moth-er with won-d'ring stare, And their thoughts were of Dad, who's "o-ver there." The

lit-tle girl smiled, then the clock struck one, As the Cen-tral called White House, Wash-ing-ton. The Pres-i-dent heard and he un-der-stood, Like the fa-ther of this great coun-try should. He

chance, The stork brought a brand - new ba - by here.

Won't you say that it's 'me,' And he'll an - swer, you'll

see; So hur - ry, please, and get him on the phone.

Hel - lo, Cen - tral, give me

France, 'Cause we want our Dad-dy dear back home.

1. C

2. C

The home.

"Well, if you knows of a better 'ole, Go to it."

Capt. Bruce Bairnsfather

Courtesy New York Public Library

(He Sleeps) Beneath The Soil Of France
(1917)

By Tell Taylor

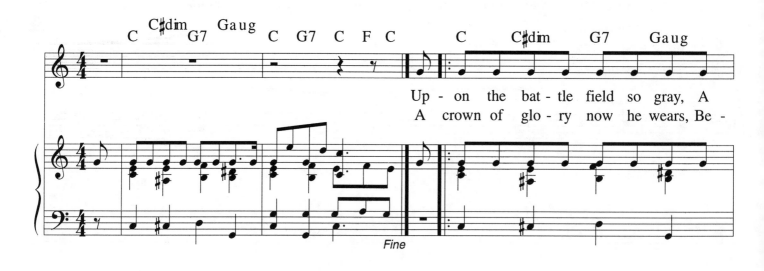

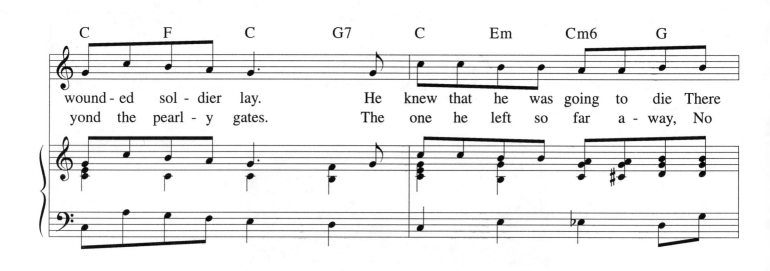

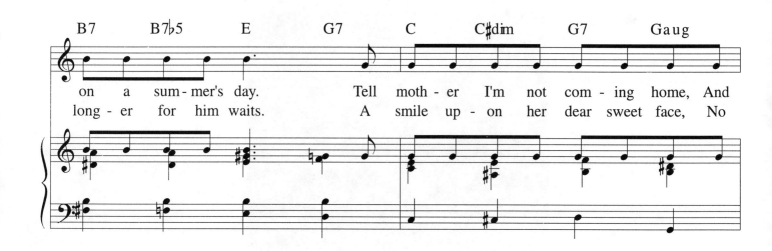

tell her not to cry. I've done the best that I knew how; I'll
tears be - dim her eye. She'll meet him on the oth - er side, A -

meet her bye and bye. *Chorus* He sleeps be - neath the soil of France, So
way up there on high.

man - y miles a - way. He left be - hind the one he loved, And a

moth - er old and gray._____ He fought be - cause he knew 'twas right to

fight for lib-er-ty; And now he's sleep-ing ov-er there, Be-neath the soil of France.

D.C. al Fine

Courtesy New York Public Library

Homeward Bound

(1917)

Words by Howard Johnson & Coleman Goetz

Music by Geo. W. Meyer

Vamp 'til ready

Some-where far a-way,
When the moon looks down

Some-where in the fray,
On the bat-tle ground,

Ma-ny boys are ov-er the sea,—
By the camp-fires' flick-er-ing gleams,—

Fight-ing for you,—
They think of home—

Fight-ing for me.—
In all their dreams.—

They're all proud to
Of the fu-ture,

104

Bb   D7   G7   Bbm

ov - er the land,— They all will hear the Gen - 'ral give the com-mand. We are

F Cm6 D9   G7   C7 | 1. | 2.
                                      | F Fdim C7 | F

"Home-ward Bound," That's a won-der-ful, won - der-ful sound.   sound.

Courtesy New York Public Library

I Don't Want To Get Well

(1917)

Words by Howard Johnson & Harry Pease

Music by Harry Jentes

I just re-ceived an an-swer to a
showed this let-ter to a friend who

let-ter that I wrote, From a pal who marched a - way.
lives next door to me, And I heard him quick-ly say,

108

109

Courtesy New York Public Library

Good-bye Broadway, Hello France

(1917)

Words by C. Francis Riesner & Benny Davis

Music by Billy Baskette

bid-ding good-bye,— Ev-'ry sol-dier's moth-er dry-ing her eye.—
brave La-Fa-yette,— Whose deeds and fame we can-not for-get.—

Cheer up, we'll soon be there,— Sing-ing this Yan-kee air:—
Now that we have the chance,— We'll pay our debt to France.—

Chorus

Good-bye Broad-way, Hel-lo France,— We're ten mil-lion

strong.— Good-bye sweet-hearts, wives and moth-ers,

*German infantrymen scrambling across the wreckage of a blown bridge
across the Manre/Aisne Canal during the fighting in June 1918. Courtesy New York Public Library*

*"AMERICAN ARTILLERYMEN LOADING GUN CAISSONS AT A RAILROAD DEPOT FOR TRANSPORTATION TO THE
BATTLE AREA."
Courtesy New York Public Library*

Over There

(1917)

By George M. Cohan

John-nie get your gun, get your gun, get your gun, Take it on the run, on the
John-nie get your gun, get your gun, get your gun, John-nie show the Hun you're a

run, on the run; Hear them call - ing you and me;
son - of - a - gun. Hoist the flag and let her fly,

Ev - 'ry son of lib - er - ty. Hur - ry right a - way, no de -
Like true he - roes, do or die. Pack your lit - tle kit, show your

When Yankee Doodle
Learns To Parlez Vous Français
(1917)

Words by Will Hart

Music by Ed. Nelson

Vamp 'til ready

When Yan - kee Doo - dle came to Par - is town,_____
Yan - kee Doo - dle he left Par - is town._____

Up - on his face he wore a lit - tle frown._____ To those he'd meet up-
Up - on his face there was a coat of brown._____ For ev - 'ry man of

on the street, he could - n't speak a word, To find a miss that
Un - cle Sam was fight - ing in a trench. Be - tween each shell they

he could kiss, it seemed to be ab - surd. But if this Yan - kee
learned quite well to speak a lit - tle French. When Yan - kee Doo - dle

should stay there a while,___ Up - on his face you're bound to see a
gets back to Pa - ree,___ He'll break a mil - lion hearts, take it from

Chorus

smile.___ When Yan - kee Doo - dle learns to par - lez vous fran -
me.___

çais, par - lez vous fran - çais in the prop - er way He will

119

Let's All Be Americans Now

(1917)

By Irving Berlin
Edgar Leslie & Geo. Meyer

Peace has al - ways been our pray'r, Now there's troub - le in the air. War is talked of ev - 'ry - where, Still in God we trust. Now that war's de -

Lin - coln, Grant and Wash - ing - ton, They were peace - ful men, each one. Still they took the sword and gun, When real trou - ble came. And I feel some -

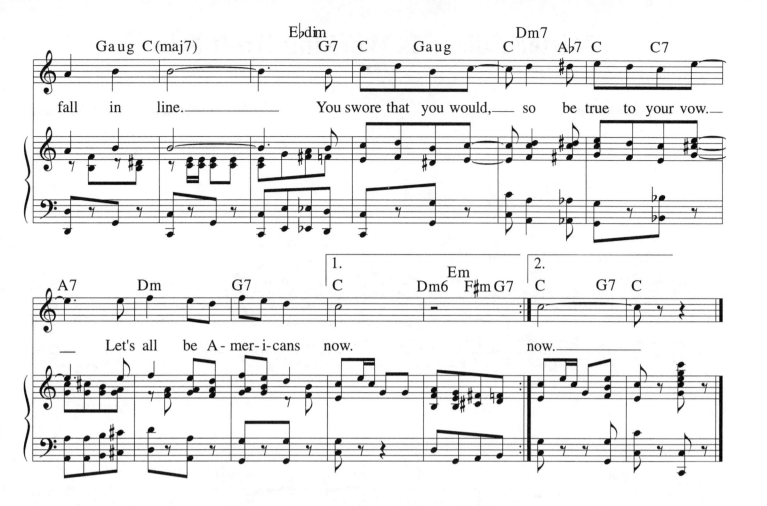

fall in line._____ You swore that you would,— so be true to your vow.—

Let's all be A-mer-i-cans now. now._____

Courtesy New York Public Library

Mister Edison Is Working On It Now
(1917)

Words by Jack Caddigan

Music by James A. Brennan

In this war the world has won - dered_____ At the
War has been with us since Ad - am,_____ And our

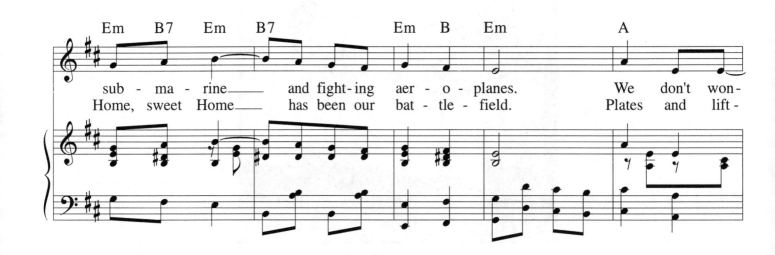

sub - ma - rine_____ and fight-ing aer - o - planes. We don't won-
Home, sweet Home_____ has been our bat - tle - field. Plates and lift -

125

126

Watch The Bee Go Get The Hun

(1918)

By Walter Hawley

There's a bee - hive in A - mer - i ca,___ they
bus - y bees at Wash - ing - ton,___ as

call the U. S. A. And it is far_____ from "o - ver
bus - y as can be, Pre - par - ing plans_____ for "o - ver

there."_____ There's a hun - dred mil - lion bus - y bees___ a -
there."_____ And ev - 'ry bee through - out the land___ is

Hun,_____ And bye and bye_____ you'll see them

run._____ We're send-ing swarms and swarms of bees

far a-cross the deep blue seas, To buzz a-round that big long-dis-tance

gun._____ So help the bee_____ to get the
Our bus-y bees_____ will get the

131

We Stopped Them At The Marne
(1918)

July 15, 1918: The Germans made their last major attack, crossing the Marne near Reims. After some initial successes they were repulsed, and by July 20 they withdrew from their bridgehead. The fighting continued until August 2. Allied casualties were about 112,000; German, 168,000. Two months earlier at the nearby Aisne River, a Franco-American force under the command of General Pétain stopped the Germans at Château-Thierry. The fortress town of Verdun was the scene of intense fighting from 1914 to 1917. Pétain was the victor there as well. Ypres, in Belgium, saw battles in 1914, 1915 (the first gas attack) and 1917. For the Battle of Neuve Chapelle, see the song "Neuve Chapelle."

By Lieut. Gitz Rice

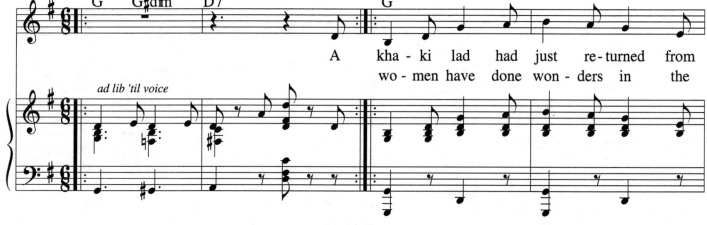

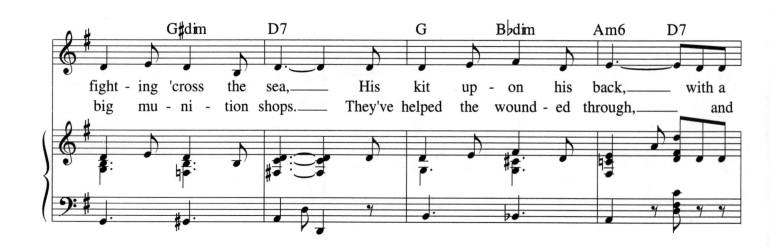

* *"Pronounciation guide" in original score.*
Actually, Ypres is pronounced "eepr."

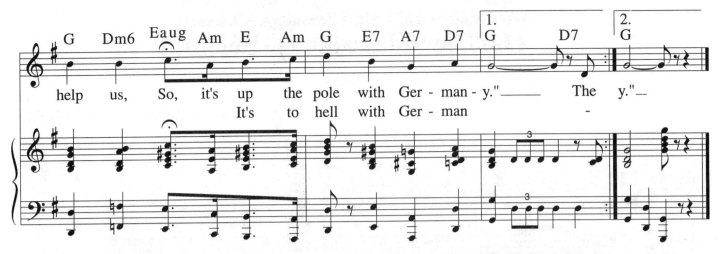

help us, So, it's up the pole with Ger - man - y." ____ The y." ____

It's to hell with Ger - man -

"Review of July 14, 1918 — American troops on the Champs Elysées"

Officiers français rapportant des casques d'officiers allemands tués á la bataille de Vic-sur-Aisne · French officers bringing helmets of German officers who were killed at the battle of Vic-sur-Aisne

We'll Sing "Hail! Hail! The Gang's All Here"
On The Sidewalks Of Berlin
(1918)

Words & Music by E. Clinton Keithley

Now, we all know the Kai - ser each
we are thro' with Wil - lie, and

day was get - ting wis - er, That some day soon he'd
knew how aw - f'ly sil - ly That he was when he

lose his lit - tle crown;_____ For he hiked a - cross the
tried to rule the world;_____ For al - tho' he whipped the

sure had some fun,____ For we have tanned the Kai-ser's

skin; And we'll sing, "Hail! Hail! the

gang's all here!" On the side-walks of Ber -

lin._____ Now, lin._____

Courtesy New York Public Library

Courtesy New York Public Library

Oh! How I Hate To Get Up In The Morning

(1918)

By Irving Berlin

The oth - er day I chanced to meet a

'Til ready

bug - ler in the arm - y is the

sol - dier friend of mine,_____ He'd been in camp for sev - 'ral weeks, and

luck - i - est of men,_____ He wakes the boys at five, and then goes

he was look - ing fine;_____ His mus - cles had de - vel - oped and his

back to bed a - gain._____ He does - n't have to blow a - gain un -

cheeks were ros - y red._____ I asked him how he liked the life, and
til the af - ter - noon;_____ If ev - 'ry - thing goes well with me, I'll

Chorus

this is what he said: Oh! how I hate to get up in the morn - ing,
be a bug - ler soon.

Oh! how I'd love to re-main in bed; For the hard - est blow of

all, is to hear the bug - ler call:— "You've got to get up, you've got to get up, you've

Good Morning, Mr. Zip-Zip-Zip!

(1918)

American doughboys, eager to see service in France, were sometimes referred to as Mr. Zip-Zip-Zip — a reference to their enthusiasm. The "Camel" was a British fighter plane (discussed in "The Passing Pilot"). "Fatimas" were cigarettes made of strong Turkish tobacco, with a picture of a belly dancer on the package. The line "ashes to ashes…" is derived from the traditional blues:

Ashes to ashes and dust to dust,
If the whisky don't get you, the women must.

By Robert Lloyd

We come from ev' - ry quar - ter, From
You see them on the high - way, You

North, South, East and West, To clear the way for free - dom, For the
meet them down the pike. In ol - ive drab and kha - ki, Are

land we love the best. We've left our oc - cu - pa - tions and
sol - diers on the hike. And as the col - umn pass - es, The

homes so far and dear, But when the go - ing's rath - er rough, We
word goes down the line: "Good morn - ing, Mis - ter Zip - Zip - Zip, You're

Chorus

raise this song of cheer: "Good morn - ing, Mis - ter
sure - ly look - ing fine."

Zip - Zip - Zip, With your hair cut just as short as mine. Good morn - ing, Mis - ter

Hello Central, Give Me No Man's Land

(1917)

Words by Sam Lewis & Joe Young

Music by Jean Schwartz

When the gray shad-ows creep,_____ And the world is a - sleep,_____
Through the cur-tains of night,_____ Comes a beau-ti-ful light,_____

In the still of the night,_____ Ba - by creeps down a flight._____
And the sun-shine that beams,_____ Finds a ba - by in dreams._____

First she looks all a - round,_____ With - out mak - ing a sound;_____
Mam - ma looks in to see,_____ Where her dar - ling can be;_____

The little girl writes to her soldier father: "My dear little papa, so that you are able to defend yourself, I have brought...kilos of iron to the salvage service. You see that I am thinking of you." The card advises: "For all information, apply to railway stations, chambers of commerce or to city halls." On the reverse we are informed: "This card, in the national interest, should be distributed free of charge. Retail shopkeepers are requested to display it in their windows and on their counters."

In Flanders Fields The Poppies Grow
(1918)

The author of this poem, an officer in the Canadian army, died in France on January 28, 1918, after four years of service on the western front. The poem, which achieved great popularity, was set to music by a number of composers. John Philip Sousa's moving setting heightens the tragic mood of McCrae's lines.

Words by Lieut. Col. John McCrae   **Music by John Philip Sousa**

In Flan-ders fields the pop-pies grow, the pop-pies grow, the pop-pies grow_____ Be-tween the cross-es, row on row, row on row, That mark the place, and in the sky, The larks, still brave-ly sing - ing fly, Scarce

heard a - mid the guns be - low.

We are the dead; short days a - go We lived, felt dawn, saw sun - set glow,

Loved and were loved, and now we lie In Flan - ders fields

In Flan - ders fields

bold and rugged

153

On The Somme Front
(1918)

The battles along the Somme River were a protracted series of Franco-British offensives during the latter half of 1916. On the morning of July 1, after an intense artillery bombardment of the German defenses, the British infantry went over the top in close-packed waves at a slow walk in strict alignment. They had not learned their lessons during the French and Indian War and at Lexington and Concord. They were mowed down by German machine guns. By July 15 the offensive had degenerated into a campaign of attrition. On September 15 the French launched an attack designed to take the pressure off the British. Then the weather turned rainy and "General Mud" stalled the advance. When the weather cleared up, the last assault was undertaken on November 13. Gains were measured in yards while casualties were counted in thousands.

Words by Joseph O'Connor   **Music by Private J. Tavender**

The U. S. A. gave up her ver-y best__ sons, To take those Ger-mans'__
Can-a-da gave up their fin-est men to fight, To teach those Prus-sians that

trench-es and guns; While sis-ters and broth-ers so fond and true,
Right__ is Might; While mo-thers and wives dear, so fond and true,

bul - lets they tear the stars from the skies, And bombs are burst - ing while the gas - es rise. When that war is won, what will the Moth - er - land say, For the boys that fought for you and me,— On the Somme— front, the Somme front,———— so far a - way. Oh, way.

Oh! Frenchy

(1918)

Words by Sam Erlich

Music by Con Conrad

Ro - sie Green was a vil - lage queen, who en - list - ed as a nurse; She
Ro - sie Green mar - ried sol - dier Jean when his fur - lough time ar - rived; She

wait - ed for a chance, And left for France with an am - bu - lance.
said, "Go pack your grip. We'll take a trip on a big steam - ship."

Ros - ie Green met a chap named Jean, a sol - dier from Pa - ree. When
Ro - sie Green took her sol - dier Jean down home some - where in Maine. They

he said, "Par - lez vous, my pet?" She said, "I will, but not just yet."
say her rur - al Pa and Ma re - fused to do that oo la la.

When he'd speak in French to her, she'd an - swer lov - ing - ly, "Oh!
But when she's a - lone with him, you'll hear this same re - frain, "Oh!

Chorus

French - y,____ Oh, French - y, French - y,____ Al - though your lan - guage is so

see,_____ But when you la la la la la la, Oh, French-y,

save your la la la's for me." me."_____

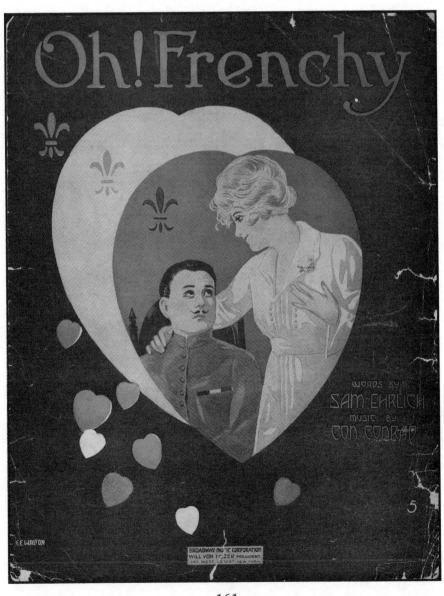

Would You Rather Be A Colonel
With An Eagle On Your Shoulder,
Or A Private With A Chicken On Your Knee?

(1918)

Words by Sidney D. Mitchell

Music by Archie Gottler

Once I heard a fa-ther ask his sol-dier son,—
Ev-'ry night you find some pri-vate in the park,—

"Why can't you ad-vance, like oth-er boys have done?—
Spoon-ing on a bench where it is nice and dark.—

163

col - 'nel with an ea - gle on your shoul - der, or a pri - vate with a
col - 'nel with an ea - gle on your shoul - der, or a pri - vate with a

1.
chick - en on your knee?"⸺

2.
knee?⸺

chick - en on your

Courtesy New York Public Library

The Alcoholic Blues

(1919)

Words by Edward Laska

Music by Al. Von Tilzer

So long high-ball, so long gin.__ Oh, tell me when you com-in' back a-gin?__

Blues,__ I've got the blues,__ Since they am-pu - ta - ted my booze.

Lord-y, Lord - y, war is...well,__ You know, I don't have to tell.__

Oh,__ I've got the al - co-hol - ic blues,__ some_ blues.__ blues.

168

KNIGHTS OF THE AIR

LOOK HINDENBURG! MY GERMAN HEROES!

How Ya Gonna Keep 'Em Down On The Farm?
(After They've Seen Paree)

(1919)

Words by Sam M. Lewis & Joe Young
French lyrics by Jerry Silverman

Music by Walter Donaldson

"Reu - ben, Reu - ben, I've been think - ing," Said his wife - y dear;_____ "Now that all is peace - ful and calm,_____ The

"Reu ben, Reu - ben, you're mis - tak - en," Said his wife - y dear:_____ "Once a farm - er, al - ways a jay;_____ And

170

boys will soon be back on the farm." — Mis- ter Reu- ben
farm- ers al- ways stick to the hay." — "Moth- er Reu- ben,

start- ed wink- ing, And slow- ly rubbed his chin; — He
I'm not fak- in', Tho' you may think it strange; — But

pulled his chair up close to moth - er, And he asked her with a
wine and wom- en play the mis - chief With a boy who's loose with

Chorus

grin: — "How ya gon- na keep 'em down on the farm, —
change. — "Com- ment vont ils rest- er là bas à la ferme, —

171

172

They'll nev - er want to see a rake or plow,— And who the
Ils n'vou - dront ja - mais plus tou - cher leur bêche,— Et dit - es

deuce can par - ley vous a cow?— How ya gon - na keep 'em
moi, qui veut par - ler aux vaches?— Com - ment vont ils rest - er là

down on the farm,— Af - ter they've seen— Pa -
bas à la ferme,— Quand ils ont vu— Pa -

ree?"— ree?"—
ris?"— ris?"—

Neuve Chapelle

The Battle of Neuve Chappelle began on March 10, 1915. It was the first British offensive against the Germans after the advent of trench warfare. By March 12 both sides had suffered some 12,000 casualties for a British advance of about 1,000 yards. British commander Sir John French, in an attempt to explain the anti-climax of the result, said he was short of shells and blamed the government. The politicians, in their turn, blamed the "idle, drunken munitions workers," and ruled that public houses must close in the afternoon to make sure that workers got back to work after lunch — leading to the persistent feeling that "anyone who feels thirsty in England in the afternoon is still paying the price for the Battle of Neuve Chapelle."

For— when we land-ed in Bel - gium, the girls— all danced with joy.—— Says

one un-to the oth - er, "Here comes— an Ir - ish boy."—— Then it's

fare thee well, dear moth - er, we'll do— the best we can.—— For you

all__ know well__ that Neuve Cha-pelle was won by an Ir - ish-man.__

Chorus: Then here's good luck to the Rifles, the Inniskillings too,
The Royal Irish Fusiliers and the Royal Artillery, too.
For side by side they fought and died as noble heroes can,
And you all know well that Neuve Chapelle
Was won by an Irishman.

Said Von Kluck* unto the Kaiser, "What are we going to do?
"We're going to meet those Irishmen — those men we never knew."
Says the Kaiser unto old Von Kluck, "We'll do the best we can,
"But I'm telling you true that Waterloo was won by an Irishman." *Chorus*

German General Alexander Von Kluck (1846-1934)

Courtesy New York Public Library

Courtesy New York Public Library

Diggin'

The involvement of the United States in the war caused a quandary for African Americans, who were hesitant to serve in the army of a country that denied them basic civil rights. Many black men, however, felt it was their patriotic duty to enlist. Due to racist policies within the army, most black troops were assigned to support details — tasks such as kitchen work, supply duties, and the eternal diggin'.

Sharpen up my shovel,
And shine up my pick,
'Cause I can't scratch this hard, cold ground
With a crooked stick. *Chorus*

Motor trucks and caissons
Cut a mighty trench.
Have to pile the metal on
For these poor damn French. *Chorus*

Deep-Sea Blues

Ev - 'ry - bod - y 'cept me. Drop 'em ov - er - board,
All these sol - diers and me, Goin' to help the whites

load - ed down with lead._____ While we're at sea.___ Oh,
make the Kai - ser dance,_____ Just wait and see.___ Oh,

Courtesy New York Public Library

When I Lay Down

The "ten thousand plunkers" were the ten thousand dollars' worth of life insurance that the U.S. paid out to the beneficiary of a soldier who lost his life as a result of combat.

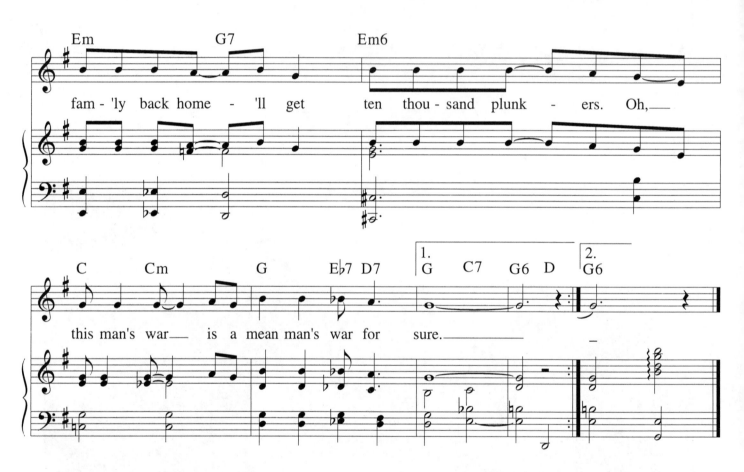

I only want to live, but I know I must die.
The fun I'll have be in the sweet bye and bye.
Oh, this man's war is a mean man's war for sure.

All of those mamas back home are a-pinin'
For a papa like me when the moon is a-shinin'.
Oh, this man's war is a mean man's war for sure.

Can't think about livin' when you're bound to die.
Can't think about lovin' when the Heinie's nearby.
Oh, this man's war is a mean man's war for sure.

Findin' out every day how to be a fighter,
I'm totin' my gun but my pack's gettin' lighter.
Oh, this man's war is a mean man's war for sure.

There's a sniper over yonder in what's left of a tree,
But he'll be a snipin' son-of-a-gun before he ever snipes me.
Oh, this man's war is a mean man's war for sure.

"Army Medical Examiner: 'At last a perfect soldier!'"

Courtesy New York Public Library

The Passing Pilot

This song is based on the ballad "The Dying Hobo," who breathes his last "Beside a western water tank." The "Belgian 'staminet" (*estaminet*) is a bar. The "busted Camel" is the Sopwith Camel, a single-seat British fighter with an unfortunate tendency to fall apart in flight or to go into uncontrollable spins. The "Spad" was a French single-seater. The "Flaming Four" refers to a British-American two-seater — the DH-4.

Be - side a Bel - gian 'stam - i - net when the smoke had cleared a - way, Be -

neath a bust - ed Cam - el, its form - er pi - lot lay. His

throat was cut by the brac - ing wire, the tank had hit his head, And

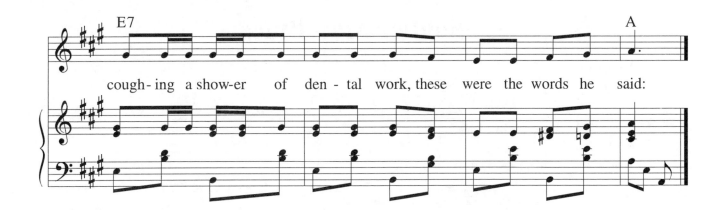

cough-ing a show-er of den - tal work, these were the words he said:

"Oh, I'm going to a better land — they jazz there every night;
The cocktails grow on bushes, so everyone stays tight.
They've torn up all the calendars, they've busted all the clocks,
And little drops of whisky come trickling through the rocks."

The pilot breathed these last few gasps before he passed away:
"I'll tell you how it happened. My flippers didn't stay.
My motor wouldn't hit at all, the struts were far too few;
A bullet hit the gas tank, and the gas came leaking through."

"Oh, I'm going to a better land, where the motors always run;
Where the eggnog grows on the eggplant, and the pilots grow a bun.
They've got no Sops, they've got no Spads, they've got no Flaming Fours,
And little frosted juleps are served at all the stores."

Courtesy New York Public Library

Soldier Man Blues

I'd rather be a-pimpin' for one-eyed Kate,
And do a first-class job at a cut-price rate,
Than tote a gun in this man's war,
Or drive a noisy motorcycle side car. *Chorus*

Now, Lizzie's a gal without much style,
But you should see those papas caper when she
   puts out her smile.
While, one-eyed Kate is full o' speed,
And she bends in the middle like a broken reed. *Chorus*

Steam train standin' on the railroad track,
Couldn't go forward so he had to go back.
Steam-train man was a-singin' sad,
'Cause his engine acted up so bad. *Chorus*

Possum hangin' on a hickory limb —
Moon was a-shinin' down on him.
Possum simply ain't no use,
Less he's floatin' in a puddle o' pot liquor juice.
   Chorus

Scratch Your Lousy Back

Scratch your lousy back, scratch your lousy back,
Keep your head down in the trench,
Or you're never goin' to see that little high brown wench.
Scratch your lousy back.

Scratch your lousy back, scratch your lousy back.
Whenever you hear the rattlin' of bully beef tins,*
You better grab for gas mask and be sorry for your sins.
Scratch your lousy back.

The signal of a German gas attack

Mister French Railroad Man

This song was collected in France by Lieutenant John Jacob Niles, an American aviator who became a singer and compiler of folk songs. In his 1927 book, *Singing Soldiers,* Niles explains the word "Bush" in the chorus of the song by relating the following yarn told to him by a black soldier who had served on the front lines: "Now boy, dis here French army is a whale of a fightin' machine.... Dey drinks a lot of tea but dey does fight.... An' de Italians, *an'* de Austrians, *an'* de Belgians, *an'* de Germans wid dose machine guns dat shoot so slow and go in so deep. But Mister, let me tell you dis one thing.... If ever you have to go out yonder and have to fight in dis war like I did...take my word for de truth and look out for dose Bush — look out for dose Bush, dey is hell." Niles adds: "The storyteller thought the so-called Boche [French slang for Germans], mispronounced 'Bush,' were an entirely different army."

French rail-road man,___ where you tak-in' us to?___ Goin' to take you up for the

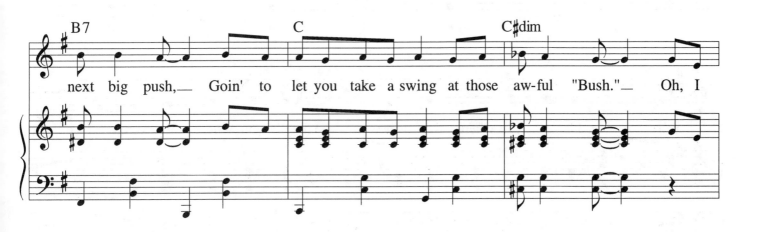

next big push,___ Goin' to let you take a swing at those aw-ful "Bush."___ Oh, I

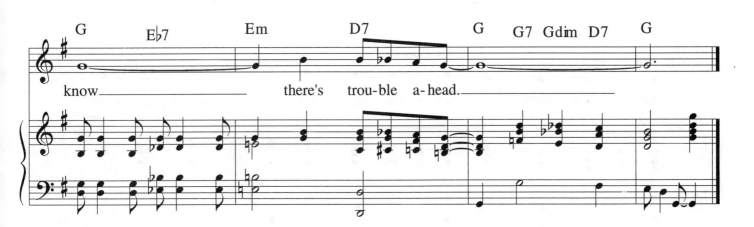

know___ there's trou-ble a-head.___

Ride all night and ride all day —
Got to stand up straight 'cause there's no place to lay. *Chorus*

Forty men and eight army horses —
Goin' to come back home with some nice German crosses. *Chorus*

If I get home to the land of the free,
Pullman train'll be the place for me. *Chorus*

Mister Engineer, won't you please haul your freight,
My feet is singin' a hymn of hate. *Chorus*

Oh, I know there's trouble up yonder ahead,
But it wouldn't much matter if I could lay my head. *Chorus*

I'll Tell You Where They Were

If you want to know where the gen-e-rals were, I'll tell you where they were, I'll tell you where they were, I'll tell you where they were.— If you want to know where the gen-e-rals were, I'll tell you where they were; Back in gay Pa - ree! How do you know?

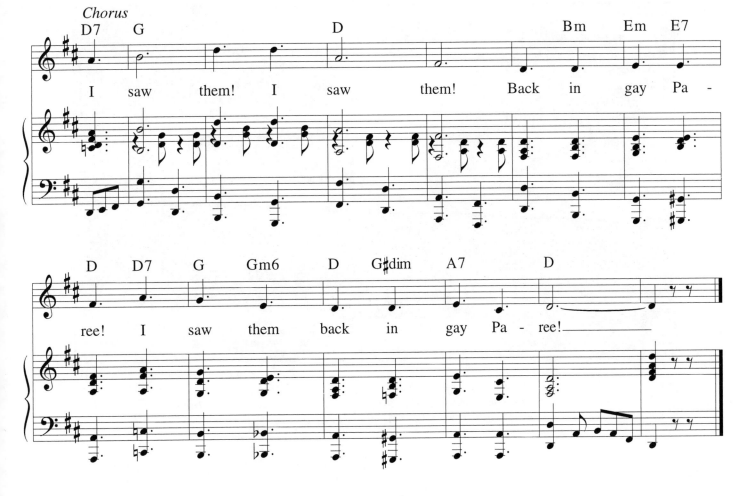

Similarly

If you want to know where the colonels were…
Way behind the lines…. *Chorus*

If you want to know where the majors were…
Playing with the mademoiselles…. *Chorus*

If you want to know where the captains were…
Down in the deep dugout…. *Chorus*

If you want to know where the lieutenants were…
Shivering in their boots…. *Chorus*

If you want to know where the sergeants were…
Drinking the privates' rum…. *Chorus*

If you want to know where the corporals were…
Sleeping in their bunks…. *Chorus*

If you want to know where the privates were…
Up to their necks in mud…. *Chorus*

"View of some of the boys of Co. D. 111th Infantry wearing German civilian clothes taken from the ruins of the town of Thiacourt which for four years was occupied by germans. Cpl. Harry L. Kinsey playing German Bass Violin and Pvt. Nat D. Gorman and Pvt. Leason Shoemaker. Showing the boys running for shelter and dropping to the ground as German shells burst nearby, Thiacourt, Meurthe et Moselle, France Oct. 25, 1918."
Courtesy New York Public Library

Courtesy New York Public Library

190

I Don't Want Anymore France

Gave my-self to Un-cle Sam, Now I'm not worth a good god_ damn.

Chorus

I don't want an-y-more France;— Je-sus, I want to go home.

When I get a chance to do my stuff,
I'll strangle some German 'til he hollers "nuff."
Chorus

I brought my razor from the other side,
And I hope to whet that blade on the Kaiser's hide.
Chorus

Dices don't love their papa no more,
Since we left that United shore.
Chorus

My gal up and called my bluff —
And brother, did I do my stuff.
Chorus

Officers, they live up on the hill —
We live down in the muck and swill.
Chorus

I got a gal — her name is May —
She holds me tight most all o' the day.
Chorus

Pay day, won't you please come 'round —
I want to take a trip to Chateauroux town.
Chorus

Soldier boy, don't you miss your aim,
'Cause when Heinie gets your range, it's going to be a shame.
Chorus

Don't waste your time wonderin' if every shell's a dud —
'Cause it only takes one to curdle your blood.
Chorus

If you don't want your bones to fertilize,
Better sing out your prayers and don't tell God no lies.
Chorus

Hinky Dinky, Parley-Voo?

Ma - de - moi - selle from gay Pa - ree, Par - ley - voo?

Ma - dem - oi - selle from gay Pa - ree, Par - ley - voo?

Ma - dem - oi - selle from gay Pa - ree, You cer - tain - ly did play hell with me

Hin - ky din - ky, par - ley - voo?

Mademoiselle from Armentières, parley-voo?
Mademoiselle from Armentières, parley-voo?
Mademoiselle from Armentières,
She hasn't been kissed in forty years —
Hinky dinky, parley-voo?

Courtesy New York Public Library

Similarly

The sergeant-major from Armentières…
He broke the spell of forty years….

Oh, landlord, have you a daughter fair…
To wash a soldier's underwear….

Oh, yes, I have a daughter fair…
With lily-white skin and golden hair….

Mademoiselle from St. Nazaire…
She never heard of underwear….

Mademoiselle who comes from Brest…
She's just the same as all the rest….

Mademoiselle from Orléans…
She gypped me out of my Liberty bonds….

The French they have some customs rare…
They sit and drink in the public square….

The First Division went over the top…
The make the Kaiser take a flop….

The medical corps they held the line…
With C.C. pills and iodine….

The American soldier on the Rhine…
Kissed the women and drank the wine….

The general got the Croix-de-guerre…
The son-of-a-gun was never there….

193

Good-Bye, Tennessee

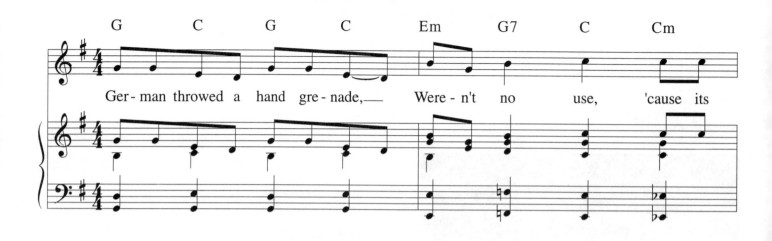

Ger-man throwed a hand gre-nade,— Were-n't no use, 'cause its

in-nerds was— dead. Good-bye,_____ (uhm hmm) Good-bye,_____ (Uhm hmm) Good-

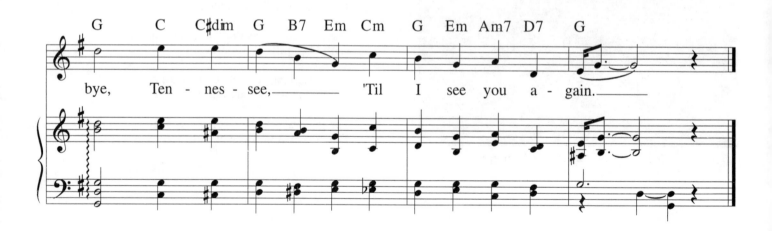

bye, Ten - nes - see,_____ 'Til I see you a - gain._____

When "Three-Sixty-Seven" went over the top —
Kaiser's army was a flop. *Chorus*

President said, "Go get your gun —
'Cause Sam, you'll have to fight that Hun." *Chorus*

Colonel says, "You'll have to plough
Trenches, 'cause this war's a wow." *Chorus*

Doctor says, "You'd better take
Something 'long for stomach-ache." *Chorus*

Tote my rabbit's foot to charm
The Hun, so's he can't do no harm. *Chorus*

I know a place in Tennessee —
Fried spring chicken is waitin' for me. *Chorus*

Goin' To Germany

Please tell me, mama, what more can I do,
Please tell me, mama, what more can I do?
'Bout all I knows, I can't get 'long with you.

Go 'way from my window, stop knockin' on my door,
Go 'way from my window, stop knockin' on my door,
I got no woman — I can't use you no more.

When you's in trouble, I work and paid your fine,
When you's in trouble, I work and paid your fine,
Now I'm in trouble — you don't pay me no mind.

Repeat verse one

195

The Battle Of Paris

As I sit on my bunk ar-rang-ing my junk, With thoughts of old Par-is in mind,_____ With viv-id re-flec-tions and fond re-col-lec-tions Of mile stones that now lie be-hind;_____ While fresh in my ears are the words of those dears, Who op-en-ly, dar-ing-ly mock us,_____ To for-get home and

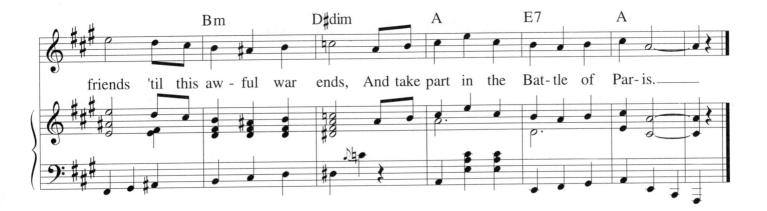

friends 'til this aw-ful war ends, And take part in the Bat-tle of Par-is.

They are strikingly neat from their heads to their feet,
And have eyes like the stars in the skies;
And fresh ruby lips like rose-petal tips —
How beautiful, you may surmise.
Now, these camouflaged birds sap the strength from the words
We are told by the chaplains to scare us.
So with vigorous hop we go over the top,
In that terrible Battle of Paris.

Now up on the line where the Big Berthas whine
And the Seventy-Fives are a-smoking,
The hell in the air fills your heart with despair,
And the gas fills your lungs 'til they're choking.
But, say, on the square, I'd rather be there,
On the Marne or the Somme or at Arras.
For with a *vin blanc* snootful it's hard to be neutral
In that infamous Battle of Paris.

The real Battle of Paris took place in September 1914, when General Galliéni's army was rushed to the front in taxicabs and buses to help fight the Battle of the Marne. Courtesy New York Public Library

Coast Artillery Song

For an "official" look at the war comes the "Coast Artillery Song," published in *The Army Song Book,* which was compiled by the Commission on Training Camp Activities. The tune is the traditional Irish "Rambling Wreck Of Poverty." Marshall French is John Denton Pinkstone French (1852-1925), 1st Earl of Ypres. He earned that illustrious title in recognition of his service as commander of the British army from the outbreak of the war until the end of 1915, and in particular for his involvement in the Battle of Ypres in May 1915. In fact the coast artillery had nothing to do with that battle, as it occurred some two years before America entered the war.

Oh, they said the coast ar - til - ler - y would nev - er go to war, And all that they were fit for was to hang a - round the shore. But when in France they need - ed men to shoot the tens and twelves, Why, they ca - bled to the Pre - si - dent to send our loy - al selves.

Chorus: Then, it's home, boys, home, it's home that we should be,
It's home, boys, home, when the nation shall be free.
We're in this war until it ends, and Germany will see
That the end of all the Kaisers is the Coast Artillery.

When British Tommies took the field to stop the barb'rous Hun,
They found their light artillery was beaten, gun for gun.
So Marshall French got on the wire and quickly told the king
That the garrison artillery would be the only thing. *Chorus*

So, limber up the sixes and tens and other guns,
And bracket on the O.T. line until you get the Huns.
There may be many plans and schemes to set this old world free,
But you'll find in every one a part for coast artillery. *Chorus*

Courtesy New York Public Library

Gee, But I Wanna Go Home

The cof-fee that they give you, they say is might-y fine, It's good for cuts and bruis-es, and it tastes like i-o-dine.

Chorus

I don't want no more of ar-my life, Gee, but I wan-na go home.

The biscuits that they give you, they say are mighty fine;
One rolled off a table and it killed a pal of mine. *Chorus*

The chickens that they give you, they say are mighty fine;
One rolled off a table and it started marking time.
Chorus

The details that they give you, they say are mighty fine;
The garbage that we pick up, they feed us all the time.
Chorus

The clothes that they give you, they say are mighty fine,
But me and my buddy can both fit into mine. *Chorus*

The women in the service club, they say are mighty fine,
But most are over ninety and the rest are under nine.
Chorus

They treat us all like monkeys, and make us stand in line,
They give you fifty dollars and take back forty-nine.
Chorus